Look Where I Live!

A look-and-find book

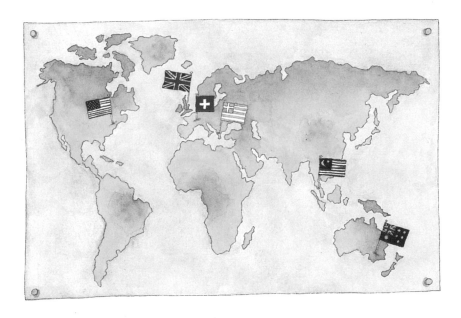

Lone Morton and Catherine Bruzzone

Illustrated by Louise Comfort

This is Angus.

He lives in Scotland.

Angus has friends all around the world.

Would you like to meet them?

Here they are!

Meilin

Sook Wing

Costas

Sam

Ross

Lily

Emilie   Pierre

Angus

Now turn the pages and discover where they live.
See what you can find inside their houses.

Costas and his brothers live in Greece.
They have six cats,
two pairs of football boots,
two little fishing boats,
three shopping baskets,
four rugs,
one football,
six pretty plates and a wooden chest.

Look inside their house. Can you find them?

Lily lives in America.
She has three televisions,
four rucksacks,
two skipping ropes,
one computer,
one telescope,
five cushions,
three plants in pots and a snake in a tank.

Look inside her house. Can you find them?

Ross lives in Australia.
He has two surfboards,
three tennis rackets,
three towels,
two beach balls,
two tennis balls,
one toy train,
seven hats and a toy kangaroo.

Look inside his house. Can you find them?

Pierre and Emilie live in Switzerland.
They have one sledge,
five pairs of shoes,
two pairs of skis,
one box of chocolates,
one drum,
three family photographs,
four wooden chairs and one blue and white armchair.

Look inside their house. Can you find them?

Meilin and Sook Wing live in Malaysia.
They have two colourful masks,
three fans,
six Chinese lanterns,
three pairs of slippers,
one sewing-machine,
two paper dragons,
four blue bowls and a yellow bird in a cage.

Look inside their house. Can you find them?

Sam lives in England.
He has two dogs,
one toy soldier,
one pair of boots,
two mice,
one rocking-horse,
two umbrellas,
eight pictures and a basket of green apples.

Look inside his house. Can you find them?
Angus is visiting Sam. Can you find Angus?

Look back through all the pages and find:
one baseball bat
two feathers
three baths
four ironing-boards
five spider's webs
six telephones
seven fish
eight teddy bears
nine clocks
ten mirrors

(The answers are ringed on pages 29-31.)

Answers

Costas' house

Lily's house

Answers

Ross's house

Pierre and Emilie's house

Answers

Meilin and Sook Wing's house

Sam's house

Word List

America
and
apple
armchair
around
Australia
ball
baseball bat
basket
bath
beach
bird
blue
boot
bowl
box
brother
cage
can you...?
cat
chair
chest
Chinese
chocolate
clock
colourful
computer
cushion
dog
dragon
drum
England
family
fan

feather
fish
fishing boat
football
football boot
friend
Greece
green
hat
here
house
inside
ironing-board
kangaroo
lantern
little
Malaysia
mask
mice
mirror
mouse
now
page
pair (of)
paper
photograph
picture
plant
plate
pot
pretty
rocking-horse
rucksack
rug

Scotland
sewing-machine
shoe
shopping basket
ski
skipping rope
sledge
slipper
snake
soldier
spider's web
surfboard
Switzerland
tank
teddy bear
telephone
telescope
television
tennis
tennis racket
them
this is
towel
toy
train
umbrella
web
white
wooden
world
would you like...?
yellow